Table of Contents

INTRODUCTION

A fairy garden is small, but how small is up to you. Some fairy gardens are planted in tea cups! Others take up a bit more real estate—say, in a hollowed-out tree stump, wheelbarrow, birdbath or whiskey barrel planter. The larger the fairy garden, the more options when it comes to incorporating hills, valleys, water features and multiple settings. While a small fairy garden might be limited to a small hobbit house, a larger one could include a whole neighborhood. Small fairy gardens have at least two advantages: they're cheap to put together and portable enough to take in the house as indoor planters, if desired.

Really, the best plants for a fairy garden are any that look like miniature versions of full-size plants. Bonsai are a natural and you can buy them inexpensively at big box stores rather than having to create one from scratch over the course of several years. Other options include calibrachoa, sedum, ageratum, gomphrena, Irish or Scotch moss, blue lobelia, sweet alyssum, dwarf conifers and a host of smaller sedums such as Angelina. Look for small plants that mimic the shapes of landscape plants:

a round shrub, an upright tree. You can even use bare twigs to represent deciduous trees that have shed their leaves.

Once the fairy garden is planted, water plants deeply, ensuring excess water drains away. After that, you'll probably have to water every other day, provided your miniature garden isn't in all-day sunlight. In that case, daily watering will be necessary. Because of their small size, fairy gardens dry out quickly, so consider using a soilless potting mix containing a slow-release fertilizer and water-holding crystals to lessen maintenance. Keep the garden where it gets afternoon shade.

If you're not sure where to start, a fairy garden kit is a good option. It can be simple, inexpensive and kid-friendly, like this fairy garden house, or more extravagant, like this fairy garden village.

Once you have the structures in place, you can add small plants and paths, streams, picket a fence, arbor and, of course, a whimsical fairy or two. Fairy gardens have gone mainstream, so you can find kits and accessories on Amazon, eBay and Etsy, as well as crafts stores, big box stores and discount stores.

CHAPTER ONE

A garden is a planned space, usually outdoors, set aside for the display, cultivation, or enjoyment of plants and other forms of nature. The garden can incorporate both natural and man-made materials. The most common form today is a residential garden, but the term garden has traditionally been a more general one. Zoos, which display wild animals in simulated natural habitats, were formerly called zoological gardens. Western gardens are almost universally based on plants, with garden often signifying a shortened form of botanical garden. Some traditional types of eastern gardens, such as Zen gardens, use plants sparsely or not at all.

Gardens may exhibit structural enhancements including statuary, follies, pergolas, trellises, stumperies, dry creek beds and water features such as fountains, ponds (with or without fish), waterfalls or creeks. Some gardens are for ornamental purposes only, while some gardens also produce food crops, sometimes in separate areas, or sometimes intermixed with the ornamental plants. Food-producing gardens are distinguished from farms by their smaller scale, more labor-intensive methods, and their purpose (enjoyment of a hobby or self-sustenance rather than producing for sale). Flower gardens combine plants of different heights, colors, textures, and fragrances to create interest and delight the senses.

Historical Background
Early history

Western gardening had its origins in Egypt some 4,000 years ago. As the style spread, it was changed and adapted to different localities and climates, but its essentials remained those of disciplined lines and groupings of plants, usually in walled enclosures. Gardening was introduced into Europe through the expansion of Roman rule and, second, by way of the spread of Islam into Spain. Though clear evidence is lacking, it is presumed that Roman villas outside the confines of Italy contained native and imported plants, hedges, fruit trees, and vines, in addition to herbs for medicinal and culinary purposes.

In medieval times the monasteries were the main repositories of gardening knowledge and the important herbal lore. Though little is certainly known about the design and content of the monastic garden, it probably consisted of a walled courtyard built around a well or an arbor, with color provided by flowers (some of which, including roses and lilies, served as ecclesiastical symbols), all of which maintained the ancient idea of the garden as a place of contemplation.

The earliest account of gardening in English, The Feate of Gardening, dating from about 1400, mentions the use of more than 100 plants, with instructions on sowing, planting, and grafting of trees and advice on cultivation of herbs such as parsley, sage, fennel, thyme, camomile, and saffron. The vegetables mentioned include turnip, spinach, leek, lettuce, and garlic.

Early gardening was largely for utility. The emergence of the garden as a form of creative display properly began in the 16th century. The Renaissance, with its increased prosperity, brought an upsurge of curiosity about the natural world and, incidentally, stirred interest in composing harmonious forms in the garden.

This awakening took especially firm root in Elizabethan England, which notably developed the idea that gardens were for enjoyment and delight. Echoing the Renaissance outlook, the mood of the period was one of exuberance in gardening, seen in the somewhat playful arrangements of Tudor times, with mazes, painted statuary, and knot gardens (consisting of beds in which various types of plants were separated by dwarf hedges). Flowers began to appear profusely in paintings and, as mentioned above, were used by poets in their verbal images.

This enthusiasm was accompanied by an earnest search for knowledge, and the period saw the birth of botanical science. A leading figure in this work was Carolus Clusius (Charles de l'Écluse), whose botanical skills and introduction of the tulip and other bulbous plants to the botanical gardens at Leiden, Netherlands, laid the foundation for Dutch prominence in international horticulture. The earliest botanical garden was that of Pisa (1543), followed by that of Padua (1545). The first in England was founded at Oxford in 1621, followed by Scotland's first, at Edinburgh, in 1667. The gardens at Kew, near London, were founded almost a century later, in 1759. These centers of experiment and learning have contributed greatly to the art and science of horticulture.

The advances from the simple medieval style were marked and rapid at this time. The English statesman and scholar Francis Bacon could already, by 1625, advance a sophisticated and almost modern conception of the garden in his essay "On Gardens." He saw it as a place that should be planted for year-round enjoyment, offering a wide range of experiences through color, form and scent, exercise and repose. The flower garden, already well established by the early 17th century, was set against a background of tall, clipped hedges and neatly scythed lawns. The taste of the time, as contemporary lists show, was for perfumed varieties such as carnations, lavender, sweet marjoram, musk roses, and poppies.

The plant trade

As interest in gardening developed in Europe, the new trade of nurseryman was established, and the trade became highly important to the spread of knowledge and materials. By the end of the 17th century, nurserymen were relatively numerous in England, France, and the Low Countries, with keen customers among the nobility and gentry for all the exotica they could provide. The catalog of the Tradescant family's private botanical garden in London listed 1,600 plants in 1656. A number of them had been brought back by the family from visits to Virginia. These early exotica from the New World included now familiar plants such as the Michaelmas daisy, the Virginia creeper, hamamelis, goldenrod, the first perennial lupine, and such fine autumn-coloring trees as liquidambar and the staghorn sumac. The work of the nurserymen thus spread new plants more widely and, as breeding skills developed, contributed to the acclimatizing of foreign imports.

Vegetables and fruits

The history of vegetables is imprecise. Though familiar types, including the radish, turnip, and onion, are known to have been in cultivation from early times, it is fairly supposed that they were meagre and would bear little clear resemblance to modern equivalents. The early range available to European gardens and, later, to those in America, included such native plants as kale, parsnips, and the Brussels sprout family, with peas and broad beans grown as field crops.

The Romans introduced the globe artichoke, leek, cucumber, cabbage, asparagus, and the Mediterranean strain of garlic to their imperial territory wherever these plants would flourish. Among plants imported to Europe from the Americas were the scarlet runner bean and tomato (both originally grown for ornament), corn (maize), and the vastly important potato. The numerous herbs in use were mostly native to European locations. One curiosity to the modern mind is that certain flowers, such as marigolds, violets, and primroses, were used as flavorings in the kitchen.

The cultivation of fruit trees was one of the most advanced skills and interests from the 16th century onward. Pride was taken in variety, and, judging by the opulent still-life paintings of the period, the quality was remarkably high. Among the challenges bravely taken up in the 17th century in northern Europe was the growing of orange and lemon trees, though this was done more for the pleasure of their evergreen qualities than for their fruit. The catalog of the British royal gardens in 1708 shows 14 varieties of cherry, 14 apricots, 58 kinds of peach and nectarine,

33 plums, eight figs, 23 vines, 29 pears, and numerous varieties of apple.

The French style

The most favored style for great house gardens in Europe during much of this period derived from the influence of the French designer André Le Nôtre, creator of the gardens at Versailles. The French style represented an extreme of formality, with box-edged parterres (elaborate and geometrical beds) typically placed near the residence to provide an arranged view. Trees were grouped in neat plantations or in bold lines along avenues, with terraces and statuary carefully placed to emphasize the architectural symmetry of the grand manner. The widespread adoption of this style among the European nobility and gentry reflected the potency of French cultural influence at the time. It was also related, on a practical basis, to the limited availability of planting materials, especially those offering autumn and winter display.

The change to a more natural style of gardening came about when, in the latter part of the 18th century, the opinion arose among leading gardeners, particularly those of the English gentry, that the formal manner brought with it a certain monotony. The increasing importation of foreign plants also brought with it opportunities for a large-scale transformation.

The plant hunters

The early importation of plants to Europe was managed through informal channels, following the increase in exploration and the spread of empires. Seeds and tubers were sent home by diplomats and missionaries, sea captains and travelers. An example of this type of collecting is afforded by Henry Compton, bishop of London, whose diocese included the American colonies. He was an avid collector, and he corresponded with like-minded experts in Europe and America and thus brought numerous fine plants to his exceptional garden in Fulham, west London. He also encouraged his missionaries to send home seeds. From one such source in Virginia came the Magnolia virginiana, the first magnolia to be cultivated. This was the beginning of what became known as the American garden, based upon magnolias, azaleas, and other woodland species.

As the appetite for exotica developed, plant collecting around the world became more systematized. Expeditions to foreign parts were organized and financed by nurserymen, botanical gardens, or syndicates of private gardeners. The botanist plant hunters thus sent out were exceptional and patient. They were required to endure long voyages and residence for up to several years in an often hostile environment. Their goal was to find the plant in flower, return in due season to collect seed, then see their delicate specimens back to Europe through varying climatic zones.

North America's potential to yield countless new specimens was recognized early: the first book on American plants, published in London in 1577, was entitled Joyfull Newes out of the New Founde Worlde and was in itself a hint of the excited spirit of contemporary gardening. The jacaranda, flowering catalpa, and wisteria were among the finds made by Compton's missionaries in the Carolinas. An early resident collector in North America was John Bartram, regarded as the founder of American botany. He settled on a farm near Philadelphia in 1728 and, in 30 years of collecting in the Alleghenies, Carolinas, and other areas of North America, sent some 200 important plants to British gardens in sufficient quantity that they became widespread there.

The extremely rich west coast of North America was not exploited by plant collectors until the early 19th century. The contemporary importance of such discoveries is suggested by the fact that, in their celebrated crossing of the American continent in 1804–06, Lewis and Clark found time to collect the seeds of Mahonia aquifolium and Symphoricarpos racemosus. Perhaps the most distinguished collector among an exceptional fraternity was David Douglas, one of the numerous Scotsmen who contributed to international botany. His expeditions to the North American Far West brought to Europe such important timber trees as the Douglas fir, the Sitka spruce, the Monterey pine, and a number of now familiar shrubs such as Garrya elliptica and Ribes sanguineum. The California annuals he discovered made a lasting impact on the color of Western gardens. In the 19th century, plant collectors began to explore South America, where two Cornish brothers, William and Thomas Lobb, gained prominence. They are credited with carrying back to Europe the monkey puzzle tree (Araucaria araucana), native to the Andes mountains; the Berberis darwinii; and the Escallonia macrantha.

Branch of the monkey puzzle tree (Araucaria araucana), an evergreen ornamental and timber conifer native to the Andes mountains of South America.

Collectors went to a number of countries in the 19th century, but the most important area was China. Its flora was more intact than that in the West, because the erosions of the Ice Age had been less severe for climatic reasons, and it had a long history of skilled gardening. Plant collection was difficult, however, because for many years the only foreigners allowed to travel within its borders were Jesuit priests. They aided botanists by sending many specimens to Paris and London. The first professional collector to live in China was William Kerr, who sent out 238 new plants. Real exploration of the interior did not begin until the 1840s. China, Japan, and the Himalayas produced unparalleled riches in rhododendrons, azaleas, flowering cherries, ornamental maples, roses, lilies, primulas, poppies, kerrias, and quinces.

The conditions for transporting plants from such distances had been much improved by Nathaniel B. Ward's invention of the wardian case, an airtight glass box that protected the plants from sea air and harsh climate. Gradually almost all regions and countries were visited, and new plants and their progeny were dispersed around the Western world. And still the search for new specimens continues.

From the 19th century

By the early 19th century, with the expansion of the horticultural trade, gardening had become international in scope. Numerous handbooks spread knowledge. The founding of new garden and botanical societies, such as the London (later Royal) Horticultural Society, helped to increase interest, encourage science, and raise standards. Such moves signaled the rise of the small leisure gardener; a floral retreat was no longer the sole property of the rich. It now extended from the manor to the small suburban garden.

Gardens in North America had generally been smaller and trimmer than their European counterparts, with box edgings and pleached trees (that is, lines of trees allowed to grow with branches interlaced to form a screen), as seen in the reconstructed gardens of Williamsburg, Virginia. The "natural" gardening style (known on the European continent as the English style), which had overtaken earlier formality, allowed wider use of plant varieties. This approach became the pervasive trend in the west, notably through the views of John Claudius Loudon, whose Encyclopaedia of Gardening (1822) set the pattern of domestic cultivation over a long period with a style known as Gardenesque. His style encouraged the individual qualities of garden elements while ensuring that together they made a harmonious blend.

The natural style was further enhanced by an English artist and landscape architect, Gertrude Jekyll. In her opinion, the first purpose of a garden is to give happiness and repose of mind. With experience derived from the richly floral cottage gardens of Surrey, she developed the idea of supporting plants with an architectural base and allowing them to grow in a free form, encouraging natural shape and creating harmonious relationships of color.

The period saw much progress in garden equipment and supplies. Heated greenhouses had been in use since the late 17th century, and mass production led to great strides in nursery gardening. The modern, bladed lawn mower was first seen in a design of 1832; in more recent times the application of the jet-engine principle led to the hover mower. Fertilizer development was also important, from the discovery of superphosphate to the devising of modern kinds of foliar feeding.

In the second half of the 20th century, interest in gardening brought in new adherents in unprecedented numbers; they were advised and encouraged by numerous publications and by television and radio programs. Though the process was very gradual, domestic gardening became somewhat more adventurous. Among the more ambitious, designs took a multiplicity of forms, from the Japanese garden, producing an austere magic out of rock and pebble, to the other extreme of the wild country garden, virtually left to seed itself. Increasing numbers of professional designers at their best set high standards to emulate. But the art of gardening still depends on a simple empathy with the needs and nature of living things. Symbolic of this essential, the spade has remained much the same implement that it had been in medieval times.

How to Start a Garden

Starting a garden can be daunting. There are all kinds of decisions to make, but a little planning can go a long, long way toward making a garden you'll love working in as much as looking at.

The three most important questions to keep in mind are:

• How do you plan to use the space (entertaining, play area, grow food...)?

• What do you envision in your mind?

• How much time and money can you devote to it?

Here are some resources to help you answer these questions and create a garden you'll enjoy.

Starting a Garden

Where to begin? First you need to choose a good site. The amount of sun exposureand access to water will play a big part in what plants you'll be able to grow.

Another good place to begin a new garden is with the soil. This may not be the most fun part of gardening, but as the saying goes: "Feed the soil and the plants will take care of themselves." You'll need to assess what type of soil you have and what (if anything) it needs. You can get your soil tested for a nominal fee at your local Cooperative Extension office and sometimes at a good nursery.

Choosing Plants

Selecting plants is one of the toughest gardening tasks, simply because there are so many from which to choose. Key things to keep in mind are your hardiness zone and your soil type, but when push comes to trowel, what it really comes down to is what plants you like and how much time can you put into caring for them.

Garden Design

Designing a garden is an ongoing process and half the fun of gardening. While there are so-called "design rules," like always planting in odd numbers, there is no garden police to enforce them. Make your garden whatever you envision. Most gardens are a mix of plants—annuals, perennials, trees, and shrubs—that is always growing and changing. Even the best thought out design will eventually need editing.

Choosing some type of theme, whether it's a color scheme, a style or a group of plants, will not only help give your garden a sense of cohesion, but it will help make your design choices easier. You can always expand from there.

Garden Tools

There are all kinds of tools and gadgets designed to make gardening easier and more enjoyable. There are a few that should be in every gardener's shed, like good pruners, but most are optional and as you gain experience, you will find yourself reaching for the same favorite tools again and again. Don't go overboard buying tools right away. Once you know what you like though, it's worth it to invest in the best gardening tools you can afford. Good tools are more comfortable to use and last a long time.

Maintenance: Caring for Your Garden

There is always something to do in the garden: planting, staking, dividing, cutting back and weeding, for instance. Some plants are more demanding than others, but garden maintenance is a given. It can also be the most enjoyable part of gardening because you get to observe the changes your garden goes through.

By regularly working in your garden, you'll stay ahead of problems and learn the seasonal rhythms of your plants. You will also learn which plants do well in your garden, which you love and which you'd just as soon dig out and give away. Maintenance is the real essence of gardening.

How to Start a New Garden

You may have visions of drifts of color, wildflower prairies, or bushels of tomatoes, but get your feet wet first with some gardening basics. For flower gardens, choose a site close to the door or with a good view from a favorite window. Place your garden where you'll see and enjoy it often. This will also motivate you to garden more.

The front lawn shown here is small, but the homeowners still found an attractive, sunny spot to add some color and curb appeal. No matter how busy they are, they can enjoy their garden every time they pull into their driveway or look out their front window.

Evaluate and Choose a Site

If you have your heart set on growing a specific plant, check to see what growing conditions it requires. Vegetables will need at least six hours of sun exposure a day. The same goes for most flowering plants. However, there are still many to choose from for a partially shaded site. If you want to start a garden where there is mostly shade, your choices are going to be more limited but not prohibitive.

The folks in this picture have a partially shaded front entrance. They could easily add a small garden along the walkway where they could enjoy it, making their entrance more of a focal point.

Also, take into consideration when the sun hits your site. The afternoon sun will be hotter and more drying than the morning sun. Many plants turn their faces toward the sun, so if your view of the garden is from a west window, your flowers may face away from you in the afternoon. Evaluate other elements of exposure such as high, drying winds or heavy foot traffic.

Once you know where you'd like to try your first garden, you must use a hose or extension cord to try laying it out on the ground. Figure out the space it will take up.

Examine the Soil

Once you know where you want to plant, it's time to check the soil. Soil testing is the least glamorous part of gardening, but the most important. At the very least, check your soil's pH. This will tell you how acid or alkaline your soil is. Plants cannot take up nutrients unless the soil's pH is within an acceptable range. Most plants like a somewhat neutral pH, 6.2 to 6.8, but some are even more particular than that. If you are growing plants from the nursery, check the plant tag for specifics. If no pH preference is listed, a neutral range is fine.

You may also want to check the texture of your soil or even the nutrients and minerals in it. You can have that done at your local Cooperative Extension office and some nurseries. Soil texture refers to whether it is sandy, heavy clay, rocky, or the ideal sandy loam. Whatever the texture, it can be improved with the addition of organic matter such as compost.

Prepare the Bed

This is no one's favorite garden chore, but there's no way around it. Your chosen site will probably have grass on it or at least weeds. These must be cleared somehow before you can plant anything. Tilling without removing the grass or weeds is best done in the fall so that the grass will have a chance to begin decomposing during the winter. Even so, you will probably see new grass and weeds emerging in the spring. It's better to either remove the existing vegetation completely or to smother it.

A sharp flat-edged spade can be used to slice out the sod. If you have poor soil and need to amend it with organic matter or other nutrients, removing the sod may be your best bet so that you can till in the amendments.

Removing sod can be heavy work, and you wind up losing good topsoil along with the sod. If your soil is in relatively good shape, it is possible to leave the grass in place and build on top of it. Place a thick layer (eight to 10 sheets) of newspaper over the garden bed and wet it thoroughly. Then cover the newspaper with 4 to 6 inches of good soil. The newspaper will eventually decompose, and the turf and weeds will be smothered. There may be some defiant weeds that poke through, but not so many you can hand weed them.

Starting with good soil means you won't have to add a lot of artificial fertilizer to your garden. If you've fed the soil with amendments, the soil will feed your plants.

Choosing What You'd Like to Grow

This is harder than you might think. If you are starting small, you have to limit yourself to a handful of plants. If you are growing vegetables, you must start with what you like to eat and what you can't find fresh locally. Corn takes a lot of space and remains in the garden a long time before it's ready to be eaten. If you have corn farms nearby, you might want to use your small garden for vegetables that give a longer harvest such as tomatoes, lettuce, and beans.

Flower gardens can be even harder. Start with what colors you like. Rather than basing your dream on a photograph from a magazine, take a look at what your neighbors are growing successfully. They may even be able to give you a division or two.

Take a walk around a couple of garden centers and read the plant labels. Then play with combining the plants that strike your eye until you find a combination of three to five plants that please you. Make sure all the plants have the same growing requirements (sun, water, pH, etc.) and that none of them are going to require more care than you can give them.

Keep the variety of plants limited. It makes a better composition to have more plants of fewer varieties than to have one of this and one of that.

Planting

Sometimes you have to plant when you have the time, even if that's high noon on a Saturday. But the ideal time to plant is on a still, overcast day. The point is, stress your new plants as little as possible.

• Water the plants in their pots the day before you intend to plant.

• Don't remove all the plants from their pots and leave them sitting in the sun for the roots to dry out.

• If the roots are densely packed or growing in a circle, tease them apart so they will stretch out and grow into the surrounding soil.

• Bury the plant to the depth it was in the pot. Too deep and the stem will rot. Too high and the roots will dry out.

• Don't press down hard on the plants as you cover them. Watering will settle them into the ground.

• Water your newly planted garden as soon as it is planted and make sure it gets at least 1 inch of water per week. You may have to water more often in hot, dry summers. Let your plants tell you how much water they need. Some wilting in noonday sun is normal. Wilting in the evening is stress.

Mulch

You hear a lot about mulching lately, but it does make a major difference in a garden. Mulch conserves water, blocks weeds, and cools the soil. Organic mulches such as shredded or chipped bark, compost, straw, and shredded leaves will also improve the soil's quality.

Plastic mulches are nice in a vegetable garden to heat the soil around warm-season crops such as tomatoes, peppers, melons, and squash.

Whatever mulch you choose, apply it soon after planting, before new weeds sprout. Apply a 2- to 4-inch-thick layer of mulch, avoiding direct contact with the plant stems. Piling mulch around the stem can lead to rotting and can provide cover for munching mice and voles.

Label Your Plants and Keep Garden Records

Keep a record of what you have planted or, better yet, keep the labels that came with your plants. This will help answer any questions about what the plant may need if it starts looking poorly and will remind you next year of what you liked and what didn't work. It also helps to take pictures and label them. You'll remember color combinations and favorite plants.

If you start a garden journal, you can also record how plants perform, when flowers are in bloom, how large the harvest was, and all kinds of information that will help you make a better garden next year.

What to Expect With Garden Maintenance

Hopefully, when you were selecting plants, you did some background checking and didn't select too many prima donnas. All plants are going to require some maintenance. The idea that perennial plants require less maintenance than annuals is wrong.

• At the very least, your plants will require one inch of water a week. If it rains regularly, that is good for you. If it does not, don't let your plants get drought-stressed. Once a plant is stressed, it will not recover during that growing season.

• There will also be some weeding to do. Weed seeds come from all kinds of sources: wind, birds, soil on shoes, etc.

• Deadheading or removing the spent blossoms from your flowers will keep them blooming longer and looking fresher. Vegetables will produce more if you keep harvesting while young.

• Some taller plants may need to be staked to keep from flopping.

It may happen that one of your choices isn't happy and dies. Move on and replace it with something else.

Things to Know About Starting a Garden from Scratch

Gardening can easily become a lifelong hobby with no limit to the knowledge you can develop. But there are some basic skills you will need right from the beginning as you create your first planting bed. Here are nine gardening aspects to help you get started.

Grass Removal

Establishing a new garden bed often means sacrificing a portion of the lawn. You can kill grass (or other ground cover) with chemicals, though this is often harmful for you and the environment. There also are several effective organic methods of removing grass and the roots that go along with it.

Sheet Mulching (Layering)

Known as sheet mulching or layering, this method involves putting down layers of some organic material, such as newspaper or un waxed cardboard, to smother the grass. It can take several months, but it is typically an effective way to kill grass. It is also organic and not harmful to the environment, as both the grass and the newspaper or cardboard simply break down and can be mixed with the soil.

Start by defining your planting bed, and then lay a thick layer of cardboard or newspaper over the grass. Ensure that any seams overlap by at least 6 inches. If you're using newspaper, make sure the sheets have black ink only (no color), and layer them at least 10 sheets thick. Then, add a layer of compost 3 to 4 inches thick over the paper or cardboard to hold it down. Wood chips will also work.

In warm climates, the grass will break down in about 3 or 4 months; in cooler climates, it might take an entire growing season. Once completed, add a thick layer of compost over the top of the planting bed. Your bed is now ready for flowers and shrubs.

Solarization

Another natural method is solarization: killing grass and weeds by utilizing the heat of the sun to bake the soil to a high temperature.

Start by mowing the grass in the planting area as short as possible. Then, hose down the area to dampen it thoroughly. Next, cover the area with a clear plastic tarp that's been cut to the desired size of your new garden space. With a moderate amount of sun exposure, the ground beneath the plastic can heat to around 140 degrees Fahrenheit. This will scorch living grass, as well as weeds, seeds, and soil bacteria.

Within about four weeks, your grass should be dead and beginning to break down. You can then dig the dead grass into the soil, adding compost or other soil amendments if you wish, and plant your garden bed.

Manual Removal

Manually removing grass is a lot of work, but it is great exercise and entirely natural. It's also very effective.

Moisten the lawn area thoroughly a day or two before you plan to remove the grass. This will soften the turf and loosen the root system. Next, use a sharp spade to cut the lawn into 1-square-foot sections. Remove each section by sliding the spade beneath the segment and levering it up and out of the ground.

The unwanted grass can be placed in a compost bin or discarded with other yard waste. But be aware that unless your composting process delivers sufficient heat, some grass seeds will likely survive and might sprout new grass when you eventually use the compost in the garden.

Garden Soil

Healthy soil is the foundation that makes any garden a success, and most plants have an optimal soil type in which they thrive. Common issues with soil that can affect the health of your plants include:

o Nutritional problems: Plants derive all of their nutrients from the soil. Perform a soil test on your garden bed. If the results suggest a deficiency, you'll need to add the necessary amendments to remedy the problem.

o Incorrect soil pH: Many plants tolerate a fairly wide range of soil pH levels, from acidic to alkaline. But soil that is too acidic or too alkaline will have trouble growing certain plants. Your soil test will also give you information on your garden soil's pH.

o Incorrect soil type: The soil type refers to the texture and composition of the soil. For instance, some soil contains too much clay, causing drainage problems. And other soil is too sandy, draining water before plant roots can make use of it.

o

Furthermore, no matter how good your soil is, you can't go wrong adding compost to it when you first start a garden. Work the compost into the soil with a rototiller or by hand. Then, rake the ground level to prepare it for planting.

You do not need fancy compost bins to make compost. Once you have grasped the basic concept of layering organic materials and providing just the right amount of moisture and air, composting is quite easy. Tiny natural organisms will quickly turn organic waste into the most nutritious soil additive available.

Plant Types

As you select your first plants, there are several qualities you should understand about them. First, plants commonly used in landscaping generally fall into certain classes:

o Herbaceous annuals: These are plants that go through their entire lifecycle in one growing season. Many flowers fall into this category, including marigolds, impatiens, petunias, zinnias, and cornflowers. In addition, some plants that perform as perennials in warm climates can be used as annuals in cold climates.

o Herbaceous perennials (and biennials): These are plants that return every year, often dying back to the ground in the winter but re growing from the roots the following spring. Some perennials are very long-lived, such as peony and daylily, while others are relatively short-lived, such as lupine, columbine, and delphinium. Moreover, plants categorized as biennials can be considered very short-lived perennials. They often spend their first year developing and then flower in their second year before dying. Foxglove, hollyhock, and sweet William are examples of biennials.

o Woody trees and shrubs: These are plants that do not have the soft herbaceous stems of annuals and perennials. Instead, they have woody stems and trunks. Rather than dying back and re growing from ground level, these plants sprout their new growth from a main trunk or main branches. All common trees fall into this category, as well as many bushes and shrubs.

o Vegetables, fruits, and herbs: These are generally defined as any plant that offers edible seeds, fruit, stems, or roots. Most are annual plants, though there are some biennials (carrots) and perennials (asparagus, strawberries). Plus, some are woody shrubs and trees, such as blueberries, peaches, and apples.

Furthermore, plants are categorized according to their growing needs, starting with their appropriate USDA hardiness zones. The hardiness zone map divides the U.S. into 13 areas, and plants are assigned zone numbers based on the climate in which they thrive. The cold limit is especially important, as this denotes the point on the map where winter temperatures will start to kill a plant.

In addition to the climate, plants have specific light and water re?uirements for optimal growth. It's ideal to group plants with similar needs in a garden bed for easier care.

If there's a chance you might not remember the names of what you've planted, consider labeling your plants by writing their names on a small wooden stake placed near them. That way, you'll be able to look up their growing needs if necessary. Plus, some gardeners like to keep a journal that maps the plants and layout of their garden each season.

Plant Arrangement

In addition to understanding plant types, you'll also need to develop some skill at garden design. This is largely a matter of personal preference, but there are a few standard design aesthetic tips to consider when arranging your plants.

Size

Take into consideration the mature size of plants when you first populate your garden bed. In general, a garden bed should be organized so the low-lying plants are in the foreground or used as edging, the medium-size plants are occupying the middle section, and the tall plants are in the background. The rules shift a little with an island garden, where it can be viewed from all angles. In that case, the center of the bed gets the tallest plants, and the smallest plants are on the perimeter.

Form

Garden designers frequently speak of plant form as a guiding principle when arranging plants. This essentially means that you should consider the overall shape or outline of the plants when arranging them in your garden bed. In general, if you seek a formal look, try to use precise geometric plant shapes, such as squared-off hedges and neat edging plants. If you want a more informal look, irregular forms are appropriate.

Line

When garden designers use the term line, it often refers to the structures within the landscape or garden bed—the edges of the garden, for example. It also can refer to the directional impact of the plants. Plants can have general vertical lines (a columnar evergreen), or they can be spreading and horizontal (a creeping juniper). Straight lines and hard angles give a formal look, while curved lines offer a casual feeling.

Texture

The term plant texture refers to the fineness or coarseness, roughness or smoothness, heaviness or lightness of a particular plant. The texture comes from a plant's flowers, stems, bark, and especially its leaves. To create variety and visual interest, make sure to use plants with different textures in the garden bed.

Color Schemes

In addition to size, form, line, and texture, one of the most important considerations when choosing plants is their color—both of the foliage and the flowers. Landscape designers put considerable effort into creating garden color schemes, but home gardeners should not feel too much pressure to follow technical design principles. Simply pay attention to the colors you're working with, so you like the ultimate look of your garden.

Warm and Cool Colors

An easy place to start is by understanding warm and cool colors, which have different attributes:

o Warm colors include shades of yellow, red, and orange. They are said to excite viewers.

o Cool colors include blue, purple, and green. They are said to calm and relax viewers.

This color theory can be used to create a garden suitable for a specific purpose. For example, a meditation garden can be planted with relaxing cool colors, while you might want to plant flowers with warm colors around a deck intended for parties and entertainment.

Unity and Contrast

Designing a garden with colors all within the cool family or the warm family is a means of creating unity. On the other hand, you might want to contrast warm and cool colors. Using complementary colors—color pairs found opposite one another on the color wheel—can add visual interest. For example, purple and yellow are frequently used in a complementary, contrasting color scheme.

Planting and Transplanting

Proper planting technique—whether it is from seeds or potted nursery plants—is critical for good results when gardening. Seed packets will have detailed information on how to plant what's inside. The information that comes with nursery plants is more sparse. In general, potted specimens need a planting hole roughly the size of their root ball, along with regular watering as the roots take hold.

In addition, soil temperature is critical when planting. Planting too early in the season when the soil is cool might result in a sickly plant all season long. But the same plant will flourish when started weeks later in a warm ground.

Furthermore, it's common for gardeners to move some plants around. Maybe they want the space for something else, or they decide they don't like the design. Whatever the reason, many plants can be successfully transplanted. Follow the transplanting advice for your specific plant, and work carefully and patiently for best results.

Weeds

Weeds are a gardener's enemy, so it's important to arm yourself with some facts about them. You first should know exactly which weeds you are dealing with.

This knowledge will continue to come in handy long after you start a garden. Weeds will pop up again and again in spite of your best efforts to prevent them. There are many sources of information to help you identify weeds. Gardening books and university extension service websites often have photos of common weeds and offer tips on controlling them.

Furthermore, experienced gardeners quickly learn not everything that seems to be a weed really is one. Many plants, especially annual flowers, freely self-seed in the garden. So if you automatically remove every plant you don't recognize, you might be sacrificing flowers you would enjoy. For instance, snapdragons, petunias, aquilegia (columbine), foxglove (digitalis), and marigolds are some flowers that self-seed. But at the same time, this self-seeding tendency can become a nuisance by putting plants where you don't want them, effectively turning a flower into a weed.

Landscape Fabric

Landscape fabric is a synthetic textile that goes over a planting area to prevent weeds from sprouting up. It works by blocking the sunlight that is necessary for weed seeds to germinate. Holes can be cut in the fabric to insert garden plants, and then the fabric can be covered with mulch to hide it. Because the fabric is porous, water drains straight through to the ground. To prevent grass and other plants from invading your new bed, lay down some edging, as well.

A good place to use landscape fabric is in a shrub bed. When planting a group of landscape shrubs, simply lay down some fabric and cut holes to plant your shrubs. The bed should stay fairly weed-free for years.

Densely planted garden beds aren't as appropriate for landscape fabric. For example, if you are opening up ground for a cottage garden, the plants are usually packed tightly together.

It can be difficult to cut many holes in a sheet of landscape fabric for this kind of garden bed.

Pests

All gardeners face pests at some point. In some instances, you can take preventive measures. For example, if you know your region has deer, select deer-resistant plants. Or if you've seen rabbits hopping around in your yard, surround your garden beds with rabbit-proof fences. There also are plants that deter certain insects.

But in some cases, you will have to take offensive measures. There are natural and synthetic chemical ways to combat pests, and each method has its pros and cons. Some natural methods might take longer to work while chemical methods can be harsh on the environment.

Furthermore, it's important to realize that good gardens are naturally diverse, and there are acceptable numbers of pests that can be tolerated. Attempting to entirely eradicate one pest sometimes can open the door to devastation by another pest. Your goal should be to maintain balance for a healthy garden.

The making of miniature garden or popularly called fairy garden started way back 1893. It all began with the production of bonsai trees, which was enhanced by adding mini accessories — making it look like a fairy's haven. Of course, it is logical for the people to relate miniature figures to fairies and other mythical creatures, thinking that they are these minute invisible creations on earth.

Types of Fairy Gardens

You can create a fairy garden indoors or outdoors. However, since many of the components of a fairy garden are tiny and fragile, an indoor garden often works better in areas where the weather might destroy the plants and accessories.

Outdoor Gardens

Ideally, the garden should be outdoors since fairies are thought of as nature lovers who delight in the world's natural beauty. Choose a location where the tiny scale of the plants and décor are not overwhelmed by larger plants and the minute details of the garden can be fully appreciated without trampling on other plants. If an herb garden is already part of the outdoor landscaping, merging it with a fairy garden can be ideal.

Indoor Options

Containers for indoor fairy gardens can be any shape or size. You can make a long and slender garden on a windowsill or line up small pots on the ledge and dedicate each to a different garden area. A large round pots either by itself or surrounded by smaller satellite pots also works well.

Plant Selection

A fairy garden should be esthetically appealing, but not too cluttered with decorations. Small plants and flowers should be plentiful.

⍰

Herbs

Herbs are perfect for fairy gardens because many of them look like tiny trees and shrubs that fairies would enjoy surrounding them. They also impart the garden with a lovely mixture of aromas.

Good herb choices that are attractive and fragrant include:

• Rosemary, which is very fragrant and has leaves that are slightly reminiscent of pine needles

• Sage, which adds a lovely hint of blue-gray color to the landscape

• Oregano, which tends to spread out along the ground

• Chives, which look like bundles of tall grass and send out pretty purple flowers

• Thyme, which looks like a small shrub and works perfectly in a fairy garden

• Lavender, another herb that looks shrub-like and produces heavenly-scented blooms

These herbs can be pinched back or partially harvested to keep them from over growing their spaces. Use the excess in your cooking.

Flowers

Fairy roses, of course, are highly recommended. However, choose primroses if you want to keep a lower profile because they grow closer to the ground.

Other flowers that work well in fairy gardens include:

• Pansies, which come in a wide range of brilliant colors

• Foxgloves, which add amazing color

• Bluebells, which definitely add charm to a fairy landscape

• Violets, which add old-fashioned charm

Succulents

Succulents can be ideal for container fairy gardens since they tend to be small and slow growing.

Some good choices include:

- Agaves, many of which have a rose-like formation

- Haworthias, which form pointed rosettes

- Miniature jades, which make perfect little trees for your fairies

- Echevaria, which come in a variety of colors and textures

Other Greenery

The following plants also make lovely additions to a fairy garden setting.

- Fern varieties that are appropriate for the amount of sunlight the garden receives

- Moss, which adds a lush feel to the fairy garden with its rich green coloring and soft texture

- Miniature ivy, which can be trained over a fairy garden trellis

Creative Ideas for Accessories

No fairy garden is truly complete without a few accessories, and many items can be made or re-purposed For example:

- Create a very natural-looking fairy house out of a small birdhouse and twigs.

• Use tiny pebbles and stones to build walls and pathways. Use buttons, nut shells, or even small silk flowers as pavers for your paths.

• Place a dollhouse-size table and chairs in the garden. If they aren't already waterproof, spray them with matte finish acrylic spray to protect them.

• Small fish aquarium ornaments, like bridges and castles, also work well as fairy garden decorations. You'll find them at any pet supply store that carries aquarium supplies.

• Miniature ceramic figurines of small animals, like birds and rabbits, make cute fairy pets. These are often found in gift shops that carry other kinds of figurines.

How to Make a Fairy Garden

Landscape Preparation

1) Find a shallow container, possibly with 2 to 4 inches depth and 12 to 20 inches wide. It is the average size for making an apt miniature landscape, but the size is up to your imagination.

2) Choose a porous container with proper drainage hole. Know that when you choose a shallow container with full proportion, water can easily evaporate. Moreover, this kind of container helps the plants obtain more oxygen towards their roots, leading to healthy root growth without the risk of rotting.

Note: In case of a much deeper container, you can add more drainage holes. If you are not able to secure a container with drainage hole, you can place a thin level of horticulture charcoal at the bottom of the container and then, top it with potting soil with the mixture of calcined clay. As there is a risk of dying out of the plants fast due to the larger surface of the container, you can aid the plants with additional moisture. It is done by using moist and long fiber sphagnum moss that helps to mulch the top layer of the soil.

Fairy Garden Kits

If you think that preparing the landscape is a bit tedious, you can move on to fairy garden kits. For many garden lovers, fairy garden kits are the easiest way to start their first garden.

Generally the kits include the container for planting, soil, birdbath, a lid that can be converted as a saucer, wheelbarrow, arbor with bench, tiny pebbles to make the paths and many more. A fairy kit should have all the items required to create the beautiful dwelling for the fairies and plants together.

To add more fun and attraction to your fairy garden, you can also decorate it with fairy garden furniture. There are varieties of miniature furniture available such as arbors, tables and chairs, swings, trellis, umbrellas, benches and others. You can also try furniture sets like children playing on a slide and mama fairy pushing her baby in the swing which will undoubtedly beautify your garden more.

The Best Fairy Garden Designs

With unique and creative ideas for your garden of fairies, you can make it one of its kind. The garden typically consists of possibly one or two fairy houses and different types of miniature plants either planted in:

• Pots

• Moss

• Stones

• Pebbles

• Ponds, Rivers, and Other Accessories

But when you want to add something special to your fairy garden décor, you have the option to incorporate items like ponds, rivers, and other accessories. There are various manufacturers who produce a broad range of miniature items, which will be helpful to accessorize your little garden. You can also find countryside walk or beachcombing items.

But then again, if you don't want to take the burden and only want everything ready near your hand, you can go with the fairy garden kits. Nowadays, they are available in a different lifestyle package such as beach life kits, wildlife kits, happy life kits, home life kits and so on. These kits are helpful enough for the theme based decoration for your fairy garden. While decorating your miniature fairy garden, you should keep in mind that the more items you add and unique ideas, the more it becomes challenging for you.

Plan your fairy garden in such a way that you will be able to keep the amazing details in scale. Usually, these gardens are designed for viewing from all sides or from single side. Therefore, you need to place the taller and lower plants properly.

The best idea for the fairy garden is the designer miniature landscape that has the large open surface in order to accommodate many plants and fairy garden furniture and other items. Before placing the items of the fairy garden kits, you need to think of their ideal location.

The Fairy Garden Supplies You Need

In order to decorate your fairy garden, you should have the idea about its different supplies.

Plants

There is a wide range of miniature plants and objects that are well-suited for your fairy garden's miniature landscape such as the following:

• Low growing sedums

• Muehlenbeckia (wire vine)

• Little leaved ivies

• Columnea (goldfish plant)

- Fittonia (mosaic plant)

- Ficus pumila (creeping fig)

- Peperomia, Selaginella (club moss)

- Jewel orchids which are grown for the foliage instead of the flowers

You can consider the tiny succulents while choosing the miniature garden plants for your landscape. A good combination of miniature plants include:

- Viola

- Plumed asparagus

- Grasslike Armeria

- Tiny ajuga and

- Ivy

Always remember to water the plants with a sparkling can gently.

Containers

The main function of a miniature garden container is to hold the soil and drain excess water. In order to choose the best fairy garden containers, look for a large open surface area so you can accommodate several features for the garden.

You can try the following containers:

• Ceramic pots

• Terra cotta pots

• Hyper-tufa troughs

• Hooden boxes

• Wicker baskets with a liner and many more

Furniture

The little miniatures of the fairy garden furniture are patterned in such as way to look and give the feel like the furniture in your patio. In order to delight your child or grandchildren or any of your loved ones or accent your own garden of the fairy land, you can choose fairy furniture from natural looking finishes in colors red, bronze, white, gray and green.

Statues

The fairy garden statues are the ultimate item that will definitely increase the uniqueness of your garden. Even many people including kids believe that having a fairy garden statue around does not only add physical enchantment but also attract the fairies and other mythical creatures.

Actually the legends of fairy are associated with the charming beauty and mystifying fascination, which you can incorporate in your garden with the statues. There are different types of beautiful and attractive statues available, which are both beautiful and charming.

Miniatures

The fairy garden miniatures are the appropriate things to complement the beauty of your fairy garden. There is a wide range of attractive and adorable miniature accessories you can find in the market including:

• Birdbaths

• Gazebos

• Gates,

• Bridges

• Mini gardening tools

• Fences

• Planter and many more

You can also add miniatures such as beautiful country cottage together with your garden flowers and greenery. These miniatures have the mesmerizing beauty to create some nostalgic effects to your garden no matter whether you are building your garden for the first time or adding miniatures to redecorate.

CONCLUSION

Fairy gardens are usually housed in small containers. Think about how much space you have. If you're keeping your garden indoors, you'll need a smaller container. For an outdoor garden, you can use something larger.

Good items for an indoor container include something like a drawer from an old desk you no longer use, an old pot, or an old wash bin.

Outdoors, you can use larger containers for a bigger garden, such as large garden plots or big bins. A fun idea can be to use a wagon so you can move your fairy garden around.

Account for the types of plants you're planning on growing. Some plants may need extra drainage, so you should find a container that allows for some drainage if that's the case. Other plants can get by with less drainage.

While you'll probably end up wandering from your plan as you create your garden, it's always a good idea to have a rough sketch. This way, you'll know how to best monopolize your space when planting your flowers. Make a sketch of your container and draw roughs sketches of where you'll keep things like the fairy house, decorations, and your various plants.

Remember, nothing is set in stone yet. Think of this sketch more as a rough guide than a blueprint of exactly how your fairy garden will turn out. Part of the fun of a fairy garden is experimenting and finding fun, spontaneous decorations as you build.

Find a good location for the garden. As you'll be adding plants to a fairy garden, find a location that gets a lot of sun. Strive for an area in your backyard that's free of shade or a space by a window in your home.

Fill your container with potting soil. Invest in a quality potting soil that promotes the growth of a diverse amount of plants. Most local greenhouses and hardware stores will sell all-purpose potting soil. Pour your soil into your chosen container so the full surface is coated with a solid layer of soil. Consider the plants you're adding when adding your soil. If plants need to be buried a specific depth under the soil to grow, make sure your soil is at least that deep.